The Montefiore Bride

First published 2020 by The Hedgehog Poetry Press

Published in the UK by
The Hedgehog Poetry Press
Coppack House, 5
Churchill Avenue
Clevedon
BS21 6QW

www.hedgehogpress.co.uk

ISBN: 978-1-913499-71-6

9 8 7 6 5 4 3 2 1

A CIP Catalogue record for this book is available from the British Library.

The Montefiore Bride

A Sussex Fictional Tale based on Facts

by

Patricia M Osborne

Back in 2017 as part of my MA in creative writing I was required to take up a writing residency. I chose my local Victorian park, Worth Park, in Crawley, West Sussex. As part of my remit, I researched the park's past going back to 19th September 1888 when Sir Francis Montefiore, the first and last Baronet of Worth Park, brought home his Austrian bride.

This short fictional West Sussex tale is based on facts from archived newspaper cuttings, black and white historic photographs and filling in the gaps with fiction.

Step back to 1888 and become part of the Victorian crowd waiting at Three Bridges Station.

Contents

THE ARRIVAL - 19TH SEPTEMBER 1888

Mr Burr and I push past men in top hats and bonneted women hovering around Three Bridges. White and blue bunting shimmers in the autumn sun. Villagers grip red flags. Mr Burr and I wait with eager crowds for the half past four to arrive.

Red carpet in position, Sir Francis steps outside. I remember his Pa before him, a good man, one to respect, the Bart's inherited that gift. He escorts his child bride, 'Ice and Snow.'

Elegance in satin, her gown embroidered with pearls, she enchants onlookers. The footman opens the carriage, lifts the lady's moon-lace train. She settles onto the seat. Her spouse slides close, smiles, kisses her hand. We all cheer.

Sir Francis gestures to the crowd, confident in his twenty-eighth year, a dignified laugh but his toothbrush tash creeps up and down. As a nipper he spent hours on our farm, watching me shear sheep and milk cows, or in the kitchen with my Mary, dipping his fingers in fruitcake mix, face blanched white with flour.

Lady Marianne's slim fingers slip from his palm. Her wee face pale porcelain, nought but a young gal ripped away from her Austrian family.

Look here, it's time. Mr Burr and I, we head the procession, he's hereby from Worth, I be for Crawley, together we lead the bridal party. Blow, bellow, bang— tuba, French horn, drums— Crawley Band booms along the road. A horseman flicks the reins, the cab draws away. Red, yellow, pink blooms of swags and garlands drape across wellingtonia dark greens. Residents in hundreds wave hooray on either side of the flowered tunnel. The pair-horses ease to a halt, jog through an ornate iron-railed entrance, covered with burgundy ivy. I guide them into Worth Park.

Horses uncoupled, willing hands take over, human force pulls the noble pair uphill. Crowds cheer and whistle, flags flap as the couple pass. Geraniums, chrysanthemums, other blooms too, burnished-reds, golds, pinks and whites form welcome floral arches for the dignified duo to wheel through onto the red-carpeted path.

THE APPROACH

School children scatter
pink, blue and purple asters
both sides of the drive

THE ADDRESS

Illuminated by amber lamps, and low lights from the water cascade, I join Mr Burr on the platform to make a welcome address to the noble family. We offer our esteem and affection to Sir Francis and his beloved mother for acts of compassion to residents and tenants. 'I give ye a hearty welcome, Sir Francis, Mrs Montefiore and My Lady, earnest wishes on behalf of us all.'

THE PRESENTATION

Hundreds of cheering families follow the Baronet and his Lady into the grounds. Takes me back to the day when the Bart's ma first came, villagers merry and welcoming. Now it's time for the new mistress, Marianne. Children in white smock pinafores, blue ribbons flying from ringlets, abandon their school slates and linger close to Mrs Montefiore as she greets her son and his bride.

Polly, a puny pupil, swings her long, blonde braids. She presents Lady Marianne with a golden-orange, chrysanthemum bouquet. Her ladyship nods, whispers, 'Thank you.' Her eyes glisten like glass.

A young servant gal approaches the bridal party. She hands over a satin flower casket and curtsies. The Master grins, dips into his pocket and hands her a penny. Just the sort of thing Sir Joseph, his father, would have done.

I hobble forward, tug my forelock in respect, pull my shoulders back and take a deep breath. 'On behalf of all the estate tenants, I offer a cup of solid silver, wreathed and inscribed by residents of the district to Sir Francis on his marriage, 14th August 1888.'

His eyes meet mine. 'Mr Brown, Worth Park's oldest tenant, more than that, our friend.' He turns to the crowd. 'And Gentlemen, I'm unable to express adequate words, please accept our sincere thanks.' The Bart shakes my hand.

Lady M offers a half smile, raises a slim hand to her face for a second before turning away.

On to the final gift from employees and servants of the land. Mr Curl, the butler, steps up, dips his bowler hat, passes a silver salver richly chased. In the centre, the arms of the family, cedars, hills and a lion, appropriately inscribed to Sir Francis Montefiore, Baronet, on his marriage, from the outdoor establishments and households of Worth Park and Great Stanhope-Street, 1888.

The crowd clap, cheer and salute. Under my direction they disperse in an orderly manner and make their way to the nearby farm building where there's a feast of finger sandwiches, scones, cakes, pastries and fruit on linen tablecloths, along with cups of tea from fine china, and champagne to toast the gracious couple. Bunting and banners drape from barn eaves. On a low stool in the corner, a young woman hugs her harp while her long fingers pluck strings. A silk basquine embraces her waist. Star-lace cloth kisses the floor.

THE SERVANTS' BALL

Servant girls by day
become princesses at night
gliding the dance floor

LIGHT ON THE LAKE

Gold   and   silver   chrysanthemums   burst   open
amongst   stars

Sapphire   Emerald   Gold

s   p   a   r   k   s

fall   like   rain

man-made rainbows

fizzle   crackle   glow

rockets blast

shafts of colour

scream

flaming fountains

diamonds twinkle

fuchsia flames

crowds   gasp

multicolours

replicate on

still water

silver sparklers sizzle

LADY MARIANNE MONTEFIORE - OCTOBER 1889

Following breakfast, we sit in the garden room surrounded by seasonal flowers. My husband's handsome face is part hidden behind the West Sussex Gazette. I suppose twenty-nine is not that old, although eleven years my senior. How I wish Worth Park was not such a long way from Mütter and my beautiful home in Vienna.

'Tea, darling?' I ask.

He looks up from his Weekly. 'That would be lovely, my dear.'

I pour the hot beverage and pass him a cup. He lowers the newspaper. Our fingers touch as he takes the drink. His brown eyes lock with mine and a smile hovers across his teasing lips. My pulse quickens from his hypnotic gaze.

His mother strolls in. 'Francis.' Our moment has gone.

Staff whisper in the corridors wondering why I am not carrying the Montefiore seed after more than a year has passed since our marriage. My husband showers me with chocolates and crimson camellias, yet my bedroom door stays closed.

All three of us, my husband, his mother and me, stroll through the autumn garden, past the trees with burnished gold foliage, and around the mist-kissed lake watching the moorhens, mallard and geese wade by.

She is everywhere. I sense her antipathy. Her son, Mr Supreme.

Upon our return, I am shedding my coat when the butler presents me with a silver plate holding a letter. It is from Vienna. I rip open the envelope, read the contents and clear my throat. 'Francis, the letter, it is from my sister.'

He puffs on his pipe, smoke rises. 'What news do they send from home, my dear?'

I rest two fingers on my lips and take a deep breath. 'Mütter is sick, they need me.'

Francis taps his pipe, ash spills into the tray. 'Then of course my dearest, we must go. I'll let Mother know.'

Our trunks are packed and we take the train to the port. *The Atlas* docks at Dover and ships us across rough waters to Baden. All three of us.

Two weeks later, I stand with Mütter on the station platform in Vienna. Snowflakes start to fall. Francis kisses my cheek before helping his mother into the carriage and stepping in after her.

He waves me goodbye from the train window. The last ever sight of my husband is his smile disappearing with the steam.

ACKNOWLEDGMENTS

Special thanks to Maureen Cullen, Sheena Bradley, Corinne Lawrence, and Suzi Bamblett, for their continued support and valuable feedback.

I'd like to thank Worth Park Project Manager, Edwina Livesey, for the residency opportunity, Elizabeth Steven from the Elizabeth Steven Worth Park History Society for her help in research resources, and my MA course leader Dr Jess Moriarty for giving me the confidence to call myself a writer.

Finally, thank you to Mark Davidson at The Hedgehog Poetry Press for offering me this publishing opportunity and for being such an awesome editor to work with.

CPSIA information can be obtained
at www.ICGtesting.com
Printed in the USA
BVHW031122141220
595676BV00002B/437